rhapsody 2016
an anthology of guelph writing

Vocamus Press
Guelph, Ontario

Presented by Friends of Vocamus Press

Published by Vocamus Press
©All rights reserved

Cover image by Daniel Rotsztain
©All rights reserved

ISBN 13: 978-1-928171-41-6 (pbk)
ISBN 13: 978-1-928171-40-9 (ebk)

Vocamus Press
130 Dublin Street, North
Guelph, Ontario, Canada
N1H 4N4

www.vocamus.net

2016

Preface

The Rhapsody Anthology is an annual collection of poetry presented by Friends of Vocamus Press, a non-profit community organization that supports literary culture in Guelph, Ontario.

The anthology is a celebration of local writing that includes both authors who are well established in their craft and those who are published here for the first time, reflecting the writers and writing that formed the literary communities of Guelph during the year 2015 / 2016.

The cover art was provided by Daniel Rotsztain. The cover and interior were designed by Jeremy Luke Hill.

Acknowledgements

Thanks to all the contributors for sharing their work so generously. Special thanks to Daniel Rotsztain for allowing his art to be used for the book cover. Thanks finally to all those who contribute to the literary culture of Guelph as readers, writers, publishers, sponsors, venues, broadcasters, and in countless other ways – this collection is a celebration of all that you do.

rhapsody 2016
an anthology of guelph writing

CONTENTS

Fluid *Candace de Taeye*	1
Designated Knowledge *Andrea Perry*	3
The Pond – Mid-Summer *Kathryn Edgecombe*	5
Finishing Work *Darcy Hiltz*	7
The Tracy Arm *Michael Kleiza*	9
Woman in a Dark-Flowered Dress *Melinda Burns*	11
Dreamscape *Burl Levine*	13
Twenty-Two *Madhur Anand*	15
haiku-arizona *Elaine K. Chang*	17
In Your Womb *Heather Embree*	19
Designated Dreamer *James Clarke*	21
Young Girl Staring Out to the North Sea *Bieke Stengos*	23

This Beauty *Nikki Everts*	25
Aphrodi– *Robin Elizabeth Downey*	27
Spells the Blue *Jeremy Luke Hill*	29
Letter to My Favourite Stranger *Nina Kirkegaard*	31
Dreaming of Ed Sullivan *Jayelle Lindsay*	33
Candy Wrappers *Sheri Doyle*	35
for my boston fern *John Nyman*	37
Like Water *Paul Hoy*	39
Grief Walks With You *Rob O'Flanagan*	41
Squirrel (squirm) *Tanya Korigan*	43
The Balcony Tenant *Hanna Peters*	45
Separation *Marianne Micros*	47
Fight Night *Adrien Potvin*	49

Fluid
Candace de Taeye

Candace de Taeye has been published in CV2, joypuke, Echolocation Feathertale.com, *and* Carousel. *She also has a chapbook titled* Roe *from Publication Studio Guelph. During the day and more often at night she works as a paramedic in Toronto's downtown core.*

Fluid

Urinalysis easily read by eye. Endocrine placeholder contraceptive. Medicated racehorses often suffer catastrophic breakdowns launching petite cisgendered jockeys. Relating to, or denoting glands that secrete hormones directly into the blood. Our better selves test-strips for alcohol levels in breast milk. To pass. So many years of tiny pills, then suddenly a plus sign soaked in piss. Their second puberty and menopause at once. The beard syrup so viscous in the needle.

Designated Knowledge
Andrea Perry

Andrea Perry has lived on both coasts but spent most of her growing years in Ottawa. She has recently retired from the Canadian Armed Forces and made a home in Guelph to pursue creative writing. She has published a book-length collection of poetry called Rise *(Vocamus Press).*

Designated Knowledge

When they guessed what was near, they buried it fast,
    used their hands,
tools of timber and rolled stone. They raked up paths,
    sprinkled it in silt.
Pried open hilltops, packed it in. Sunk it to river beds,
    set it in sludge.
Peeled the fields back, and laid it tenderly beneath the
    civilization to come.
An extraordinary secret in plain under sight, under foot
    but hardly felt,
barely heard, unless one spread himself out and put an
    ear to the pulsing earth.
After they passed, only the trees knew, drew it up and
    splintered it skyward
to signal the rest.

They buried it fast but buried it shallow,
just under the lid of the world, hopeful we wouldnt be too
    long noticing.[1]

---

[1] Excerpted from *Rise* (Vocamus Press, 2016).

The Pond – Mid-Summer
Kathryn Edgecombe

Kathryn Edgecombe has been able to indulge her love affair with words ever since she quit teaching and moved to the country. She now spends as much time as possible in her writing cabin by the pond.

The Pond – Mid-Summer

Willows clutch at water's edge
    pull land around themselves
Waterweed dapples surface
    colourless flowers curl

Schools of catfish minnows roll
    like pulsing waves
Young painted turtle wobbles
    to deeper water, a comedy

Bull-rushes echo double arcs
    beneath the trembling aspens
Milkweed droop their plum
    heads water-wards

Ruffled face of pond
    a watercolour painting
Hemlocks, cumulus clouds
    frame of Boneset and Pearly Whites

Palette of cool colours, greens
    pond-water blue
Baltimore Oriole dazzles
    then disappears

Finishing Work
Darcy Hiltz

Darcy R. Hiltz grew up in Nova Scotia and lives now in Fergus. He works as an Archivist / Librarian at the Guelph Public Library. He has published a chapbook of poetry called Beyond All This *(Fenylalanine Publishing).*

Finishing Work

creates a fine powder
on my hand
from 100 grit
on baseboard
that dries my mouth
like a cracker
I somehow inhaled
and then friction furnishes
a shiver throughout my body
that curls the tongue back

The Tracy Arm
Michael Kleiza

Michael Kleiza is a poet and a long-time supporter of poetry as a judge for the Eden Mills Writers' Festival Poetry Contest and as a former member of the poetry editorial staff at Carousel *magazine*. He has published a collection of poetry, A Poet on the Moon *(Vocamus Press)*.

The Tracy Arm

It was a glacial hand that scarred
and smoothed these cliffs.

This water and ice breathes
mist that hugs the polished rock face,
curls up and sleeps in the hanging valleys.

Ice in translucent blue and water
coloured turquoise,
stand me speechless.

Remember this aftermath, this
tortured beauty.

Woman in a Dark-Flowered Dress
Melinda Burns

Melinda Burns is a writer and a psychotherapist in Guelph, where she also teaches writing. Her fiction has won several awards, her poetry has been published in various magazines, and her essays on writing have appeared in journals, anthologies, and on the CBC.

Woman in a Dark-Flowered Dress

Busy traffic-clogged road,
idling in my car I watch her:
older woman in a dark-flowered dress
follows her husband pushing the grocery cart

she sways as she walks
one hand on hip
grey-streaked black hair
pulled back in a bun

dress on solid form moving
around her solid legs, conjuring
her as a younger woman, in Italy?
Croatia? Czechoslovakia? Spain?

a romance country where
when she walked down the street
all the men followed

Dreamscape
Burl Levine

A lifelong resident of Guelph, Burl Levine graduated from Wilfrid Laurier University, taught English at Conestoga College for twenty-five years, and has offered proofreading and editing services since 1996. He has read his work widely and has recently published his fifth book.

Dreamscape

this morning I awoke,
wiping the night
from my eyes,
the sunlight cremating
the shadows of my dreams

the dawn's embryonic essence
began permeating my senses
and all too soon
the day was upon me,
already being sent into
its morning of tomorrow
and I, sentenced to
my mourning of today

in sympathy,
nature saturated the air
with its moisture
and the dampness made
my tears seem less wet

the flood now over,
I desired to leave
the ark of my sorrow,
and I did,
by dreaming of you

Twenty-Two
Madhur Anand

Madhur Anand is a poet and a Professor in the School of Environmental Sciences at the University of Guelph. She has co-edited Regreen: New Canadian Ecological Poetry, and published a collection of her own poetry, A New Index for Predicting Catastrophes *(McClelland & Stewart)*.

Twenty-Two

Nights lit up with a timer. Our programmable nests evolving new synonyms. Spring is a thermostat,

a due date, a flutter. Some products are just simple sums, but there is a harder green: multiplication

that fails to ripen. For now, well-bound prospectus, glow on a branch. I read aloud and current children cheer.

"Oh, wie schön ist Panama!" A bear and a tiger setting sail in a crate with the scent of bananas.[2]

---

[2] Excerpted from *A New Index for Predicting Catastrophes* by Madhur Anand. Copyright 2015 Madhur Anand. Published by McClelland & Stewart, a division of Penguin Random House Canada Limited, a Penguin Random House Company. Reproduced by arrangement with the Publisher. All rights reserved.

haiku-arizona
Elaine K. Chang

Elaine Chang is an Associate Professor in the School of English and Theatre Studies, University of Guelph. Her publications include Reel Asian *(Coach House Press),* De-centre *(YYZ Books), and a section in the* Blackwell Companion to English Literature.

haiku-arizona

light palpitates dark
with white plastic forks leaving
no marks on tear ducts
pressed to granular
hiss, issue faint steam in shapes
of hammers or stars.

feet first she falls on
his tongue, taut landing curling
up round her ankles.
filigree cracks climb
freeze-dried high arches, send thrills
metatarsal to rocking skull, cross-hatch
up a likeness to trees or
fishbones. nothing hurts

despite what marrow
might say. arid abysmal
adulthood crumples
air above snakes that
lash limbs and weave
brittle slippery mirages
of human women
who look humid but sound hoarse.

their stiletto breath
taps holes in hot sand.
his words sizzle, dissemble
when they land, form
pearl bead pools she now dabs
behind as many undulating knees, on pulse
points wrung uncertain.[3]

---

[3] Excerpted from "The Education of Misses Kim" which first appeared in *Han küt: Critical Art and Writing by Korean Canadian Women* (Inanna Publications, 2007).

In Your Womb
Heather Embree

Heather Embree is a trained metaphysical healing and intuitive practitioner based in Guelph. She has recently released a children's book called The Stellar Queen of Oaxaca *(Saplings Press) and is currently working on a collection of poetry entitled* Gringa Haikus.

In Your Womb

It was warm, still sad
knowing you missed dad,
lost in fantasies
of his own making
faking, waning
your love

My heartbeat is
weak
from your loss

Your silent grief
from vacant, lonely nights
suffocated me
in your womb.

Designated Dreamer
James Clarke

James Clarke is the author of almost twenty books of poetry and memoir, most recently The Quality of Mercy *(JHC Press). He is a former Superior Court judge, and his judgments have been published extensively in legal journals. He lives in Guelph.*

Designated Dreamer

>...and the dream outlasts
>Death, and the dreamer will never die.
>   – R.S. Thomas

I am your designated dreamer,
intimate like you with the history

of disappointment, steeped in the
shadowlands of sleep, one who

surfs the rag ends of dreams at
night to bring you news of your

buried self, wake you from your
dreamless bed, make you under-

stand there's nothing solid any-
where for you to stand on except

your Shadow, the dark rich earth
of your heart.[4]

---

[4]* Excerpted from *Winter with Flowers* (JHC Press, 2016).

Young Girl Staring Out to the North Sea
Bieke Stengos

Bieke was born in Belgium, came to Canada as a young woman, and has lived here ever since, with time spent in various countries overseas. She has published two collections of poetry, Abandoned by the Muse *(Vocamus Press) and* Transmigrator *(The Private Press).*

Young Girl Staring Out to the North Sea

If plankton
turns to soup
and sea creatures
beach themselves
as if they believe
life on solid ground
could save them

And if that solid ground
starts heaving
and burning
swallowing cars
in a vomit of excess water
swallowing creatures
having lost knowledge of
how to stay alive
in water

If all that comes to pass
will I remember
sitting on a dune in Cadzand-Bad
contemplating the rest of my
still very young life
and wondering
if I could forever
hide myself
in a poem

This Beauty
Nikki Everts

Nikki Everts grew up in Berkeley, California, immigrated to Montreal and spent the last twenty-two years in Guelph. She is currently working on several writing projects under the auspices of her company, Scripted Images.

This Beauty

This beauty plagues me of an afterthought
Dreamt once upon a distant afternoon
Lingers there the aroma briefly caught
Of wisdom lost and found again too soon

Flirtatious truth evades my grasping wit
But still I seek for depths unsung
As the blind man turns his face to it
The unseen warmth of a prodigal sun

Now in the darkness of a covert sky
Beauty rids all falsity, and bans
The hasty opening of an unclean eye
I stumble forth into these brazen lands

Better not to see what mind will misconstrue
Best trust the wind that brought me here
I lean upon the unfelt touch most true
And sigh for words too difficult to hear

So stir me with the waywardness of stars
Engage my sated soul with mystery's themes
Entice my halting heart to wander far
And find me once again within your dreams

Aphrodi–
Robin Elizabeth Downey

Robin Elizabeth Downey was born under a much different name in Toronto. Her collection of erotic stories, Every Way I Know How, *was released in 2015. She has long been working on a collection of poetry that she feels might be nearing completion.*

Aphrodi–

aphrodite
lifts her
terracotta
dress, reveals
aphroditus,
invites her
votaries
to change
clothing

Spells the Blue
Jeremy Luke Hill

Jeremy Luke Hill is the publisher at Vocamus Press and the Managing Director at Friends of Vocamus Press. He has written a children's fantasy novel called Lindy, *a collection of poetry and short prose called* Island Pieces, *and a chapbook of poetry called* These My Streets.

Spells the Blue

Cloud spells the blue   – the surgeons will
its vast labour,   take her left breast,
covers the dread   give back life in
of our scant selves;   percentages –

an occluded   – secrete their pills
sky recedes, haunts   subcutaneous,
the horizon's   poison to a pause
unending edge;   her potency –

its hazed azure   – mark her futures
makes opaque for   in mammograms
us the plunged crest   that should but don't
of vertigo;   take half the time –

Letter to My Favourite Stranger
Nina Kirkegaard

Nina Kirkegaard is a student at Our Lady of Lourdes High School. She recently moved to Guelph from Quebec City. She enjoys collecting vinyl records, reading, and watching movies by the likes of Tarantino and Almodovar.

Letter to My Favourite Stranger

Stubborn, my eyes live their own life
They force me to stare
You wont know

Away in your thoughts
You're already gone.
One ticket please

To sightsee your mind
Marvel its wonders
Truly the greatest honour.

When luck treats me
Your glance travels my way
Only I've unmoored you

Sorrow wounds me
I simply ask,
Regret ignoring me.

Alas I know myself
Too well. I am
Excess, I am greed.

It would not be enough
I'd always want more
Ask for your world.

Dreaming of Ed Sullivan
Jayelle Lindsay

Jayelle Lindsay studied poetry with Joan Logghe and Pat Schneider. She has published a book of poetry – Tangible Evidence – and teaches a monthly writing workshop – Writing from the Body – that references her other interests in yoga and physiotherapy.

Dreaming of Ed Sullivan

I was so upset once, I stepped on every crack
on the way to school. When I got home her back
was fine. She broke eggs into a bowl, I watched her fold
them into the batter. We ate dessert every night.
Her wedding dress had fifty satin buttons.
We had to go to bed. They watched Ed Sullivan.

Before 1948 no one had ever seen Ed Sullivan.
On summer nights, we played Kick- the-can and Crack-
the-whip. My brother got told to button
his lip. You might think I'm going a long way back
but I remember it stormed that night
from the porch, the sheets of rain would fold and unfold.

My aunt taught me Origami, how to fold
paper and they also showed it on Ed Sullivan
but we had company that night.
Horse chestnuts on strings will crack –
loud as anything. We stole the sugar bowl, went out back,
stole rhubarb, sat on the branch of the apple tree like
      buttons.

Home sick from school I could play with the button
box or help Mom with the sheets she had to fold.
In forth grade, Pamela Wilson got held back.
We were told she watched too much Ed Sullivan.
If you put Coleman's mustard and water in a sidewalk
    crack,
the worms will come up. My aunt would say 'Gooood
    Night!'

Our garden had fireflies and bats at night.
I had a blue velvet coat with pearl buttons
to wear to my uncle's wedding and my Cracker
Jack prize was a diamond ring! If we fold
all the newspapers, we can watch Ed Sullivan!
We saw an acrobat spin plates, lying on his back.

Dad worked too hard once and hurt his back.
He had to stay in bed with linament. One dark night
Mom rubbed him in with toothpaste. Ed Sullivan
aad Topo Gigio, Wayne & Shuster and Red Buttons.
The United Church had Welch's grape juice, taught us to
    fold
our hands to pray. I kept my eyes open a crack.

Now I can manage buttons up the back.
I fold my own egg whites and on Sunday night
I crack my shins on old memories, dream I'm married to
    Ed Sullivan.

Candy Wrappers
Sheri Doyle

Sheri Doyle is a freelance writer and editor. She is also the Director of Communications at Friends of Vocmaus Press. She is the author of nine nonfiction books and numerous magazine and newspaper articles. She also writes poetry and fiction.

Candy Wrappers

I tried to do something sensible,
resourceful (environmental even?)
but especially constructive
with all of the wrappers.

I hand-sewed a dress for you –
a ball gown of
waxy white and shiny gold
with a flowing
(and I know this is a bit much)
half-mile train.

What started out as a handbag
slowly became something much larger.
(I know – not practical.
You don't even like casual dresses.)

If you wear it (you won't)
you'll smell like a caramel.
People will stop and say,
"How sweet!"

I'll be trailing behind,
train held up in one hand,
a threaded needle and
fresh wrapper in the other,
caramel melting in mouth.

But let's be real here –
I won't make you wear the gown.
I'll wear it myself and spare you
the burden of my indulgences.

(This is not a confession
or an apology, although I am sorry.
This is a gown pattern
if ever you need one.)

for my boston fern
John Nyman

John Nyman's work has appeared in various print and online publications. He has also published a book-length collection of poetry, Players *(Palimpsest Press). Originally from Toronto, John lives in Guelph with his partner, visual artist Amanda Boulos.*

for my boston fern

Counting on an elevator's triggers,
I got lost on the way to the floor,
lit up a pattern like the minimal
voices squeaking through it.

Teach me what I need and what I want
more badly. Wave to beckon me
over the top like nothing ever happened,

and prepare me to praise you every sunrise
upon the look I contort before coffee, before
I fool myself into believing. Yes,

let's give our thanks to light's resemblance
and only afterwards enjoy. May we cease
our expressions like Yosemite landscapes
basted on negatives. May we float

at the height of the tops of our heads
and gaze on ourselves like a background.

Like Water
Paul Hoy

Paul Hoy is a poet residing in Guelph. He studied English Literature at the University of Toronto. His poetry is shaped by the natural landscape and the wilderness of northern Canada.

Like Water

I am tired of these directions, the lights on Hanlon,
the salt trucks on the 401, the fields of snow calm as lakes,
the tops of birch trees trapped in the swamp ice,
and deer crossings made impassable by rows of crows,
the rudeness of pavement churning into gravel,
the handfuls of stars that shine for the cold.
I am tired of seeing you cry and somehow not
going to you because the way feels too great – and
it is not until I drive back past lawns of snow,
the long silences of trees, and the traffic of words
to this small room that I see it all from here:
the spaces that great distances make and the feeling
of sleep that fills them, like water.

Grief Walks With You
Rob O'Flanagan

Rob O'Flanagan is an award-winning reporter, photojournalist and columnist, a poet, and a visual artist. He is the author of two volumes of short fiction, The Stories We Tell *and* The Blown Kiss Collection, *and the co-author of a poetry collection,* Open Up the Sky *(Vocamus Press).*

Grief Walks With You

Grief is always walking with you.
Snub it, still it stays close,
following at a distance,
or undercover.

Say hello, it says hello back,
comes along side, a hand
on the shoulder.
'I'm here for you. Are you
here for me?'

Run, hide.
Curse it as a foe.
Drink it to a blur.
Say, 'No, no, I'm
fantastic. I'm good.'

Or bring it in close,
listen to it groan.
Give it time, it will tell
you what is missing,
share the love locked
up in it.

Squirrel (squirm)
Tanya Korigan

Tanya Korigan is a poet and artist. Her work has been animated with dance and audio-visual projections by The Pins and Needles Fabric Company, exhibited as part of The 100 Notebook Project, and included in a pamphlet commemorating Col. John McCrae's "In Flanders Fields".

Squirrel (squirm)

heavenly host of dead flies fallen
    after hours of fury, battling at screens

    – or minutes: what is the length
    of a fight to the death for a fly? –

lifting feet to sky in the grooves of window
where in darker seasons the storm windows go

    like so many small pets
    waiting an eternity
    to have their bellies rubbed.

also here, in the house shuttered up four years
    a single mouse caught in a trap

a tollund man, voodoo mummy,
a babe blackened as though burnt

    or in desiccation
    shrunken to a second infancy

only scat shows that once a family or tribe
scurried these baseboards –

        now the best and worst of his or her kind
        a curled black cashew creature.

no living things passing simple since a death
        so tenuous it may not have occurred:

        newly-birthed squirrel, scald-pink, light-blind,
        its spine reaching and retracting like coral

for a mother and nest which
may never
be retrieved

        the baffled unknowing, the bitter
        blessing of not knowing,

the seed scattered to an uncertain end.

The Balcony Tenant
Hanna Peters

Hanna Peters is a Zoology student at the University of Guelph. She finds poetry in the unnoticed moments of life (the ones that sooth our melancholy), and her mind travels through these moments like a subway train in Japan.

The Balcony Tenant

The yellow urn
used to keep a plant.
Now it sits
    beside a mop
looking away from me wondering
why it's an ash tray,
and all I can say
    is "yeah, I feel it too."

Separation

Marianne Micros

Marianne Micros was an Associate Professor at the University of Guelph, teaching literature and creative writing. She is the author of the poetry collections, Upstairs Over the Ice Cream *(Ergo Productions),* Seventeen Trees *(Guernica Editions), and* The Key of Dee.

Separation

he woke up   saw me standing there
silently   beside the bed
saw another me   sleeping beside him
the me standing there   did not move
he got up   turned on the light
she was still there
slowly   fading
back into my body

I look for him   beside the bed
he is not standing there

my dream of his death come true
the phone call   the voice saying
he is gone   never to walk with me
again   never to sleep beside me

his spirit moved on   never returned

separation   this time   forever
soul leaves body   does not stand there
watching   goes   somewhere else

stillness of the dead   body a puppet
no one moves the strings of life
the body in repose
spark missing   no one can light
the fire

I am wooden   stiff
my soul stands outside my body
watching me move   through days
through weeks   without thought
or flame

she watches me sleep
slowly re-enters
a leg   an arm   a twitch of the lip
sharp pinches of pain   of joy
arms ache   legs swell   heart
speeds up   beats   a rhythm
not regular   off   beat

I buy a dress with buttons from top to
bottom   teach my fingers to push
tiny buttons through holes

a slow dress   hard to take off
hard to put back on

Fight Night
Adrien Potvin

Adrien Potvin is a content writer, poet, and musician. He is a member of the &, Collective, a Guelph-based experimental poetry group.

Fight Night

They spark some cheap exchange,
little else on the mind except blood's iron tinge
in the mouth. Little else to say apart from
buddy had it coming.

Yer flex is in flux, bud – brute
bodies, Boccioni blur,
bodied, bloodied, domed, whatever
the passerbys say.

They flail out into the street,
the cab's horn the bell,
the best friend the ref,
the road, the ring. No cops, weapons, heroes.

Blows flow blunt, formless,
shouts ring out across the flat fog.
One shirt torn, the other
just fuckin' *gone*, just like that.

Friends of Vocamus Press

Friends of Vocamus Press is a non-profit community organisation that supports book culture in Guelph and the surrounding area. It runs workshops, writing groups, and writer hang-outs. It offers resources for writers looking to publish their work both traditionally and independently. It promotes readings, launches, and other literary events in the community. It also produces the annual *Rhapsody* anthology. For more information, email info@vocamus.net.

www.ingramcontent.com/pod-product-compliance
Lightning Source LLC
Chambersburg PA
CBHW020022050426
42450CB00005B/599